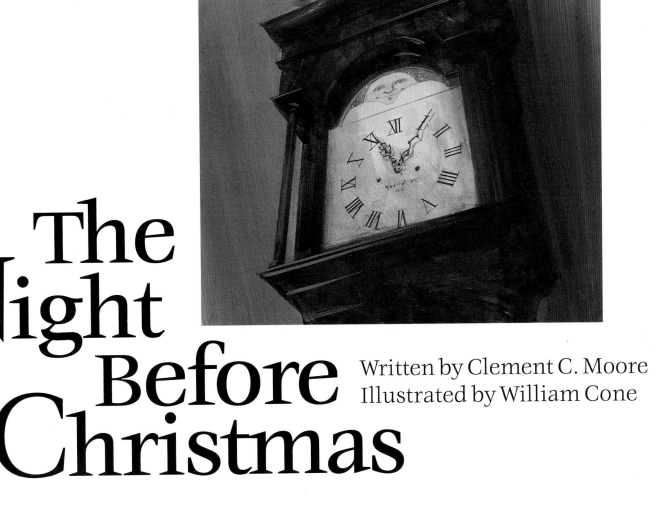

The Night Before Christmas

Written by Clement C. Moore
Illustrated by William Cone

Rabbit Ears Books

To P. Thanks for all your love and support.—W.C.

Copyright © 1992 Rabbit Ears Productions, Inc., Rowayton, Connecticut.
Rabbit Ears Books is an imprint of Rabbit Ears Productions, Inc.
Published by Picture Book Studio Ltd., Saxonville, Massachusetts.
Distributed in the United States by Simon & Schuster.
Distributed in Canada by Vanwell Publishing, St. Catharines, Ontario.
Printed in Hong Kong.
10 9 8 7 6 5 4 3 2 1

Library of Congress Cataloging-in-Publication Data
Moore, Clement Clarke, 1779–1863
The night before Christmas / written by Clement C. Moore : illustrated by William Cone.
p. cm.
Summary: A well-known poem about an important Christmas Eve visitor.
ISBN 0-88708-260-2 (book/cassette) : $19.95. —ISBN 0-88708-261-0 (book) : $14.95
1. Santa Claus—Juvenile poetry. 2. Children's poetry, American. 3. Christmas—Juvenile poetry.
[1. Santa Claus—Poetry. 2. Christmas—Poetry. 3. American poetry. 4. Narrative poetry.]
I. Cone, William, ill. II. Title.
PS2429.M5N5   1992
811'.2—dc20   92—22712
CIP
AC

Twas the night before Christmas, when all through the house
Not a creature was stirring, not even a mouse;
The stockings were hung by the chimney with care,
In hopes that St. Nicholas soon would be there;

The children were nestled all snug in their beds,
While visions of sugar-plums danced in their heads;

And Mamma in her kerchief, and I in my cap,
Had just settled our brains for a long winter's nap,

When out on the lawn there arose such a clatter,

I sprang from the bed to see what was the matter.

Away to the window I flew like a flash,

Tore open the shutters and threw up the sash.

The moon on the breast of the new-fallen snow
Gave the luster of midday to objects below,
When, what to my wondering eyes should appear,
But a miniature sleigh, and eight tiny reindeer,

With a little old driver, so lively and quick,
I knew in a moment it must be St. Nick.

More rapid than eagles his coursers they came,
And he whistled, and shouted, and called them by name:

Now, Dasher! now, Dancer!
now, Prancer and Vixen!
On, Comet! on, Cupid!
on, Donner and Blitzen!
To the top of the porch!
to the top of the wall!
Now dash away! dash away!
dash away all!

As dry leaves that before the wild hurricane fly,
When they meet with an obstacle, mount to the sky,
So up to the house-top the coursers they flew,
With the sleigh full of toys, and St. Nicholas, too.

And then, in a twinkling, I heard on the roof
The prancing and pawing of each little hoof.
As I drew in my head, and was turning around,
Down the chimney St. Nicholas came with a bound.

He was dressed all in fur, from his head to his foot,
And his clothes were all tarnished with ashes and soot;
A bundle of toys he had flung on his back,
And he looked like a peddler just opening his pack.

His eyes how they twinkled! his dimples how merry!

His cheeks were like roses, his nose like a cherry!

His droll little mouth was drawn up like a bow,

And the beard of his chin was as white as the snow;

The stump of a pipe he held tight in his teeth,
And the smoke it encircled his head like a wreath;
He had a broad face and a little round belly,
That shook when he laughed, like a bowlful of jelly.

He was chubby and plump,
a right jolly old elf,
And I laughed when I saw him,
in spite of myself;
A wink of his eye
and a twist of his head
Soon gave me to know
I had nothing to dread.

He spoke not a word, but went straight to his work,
And filled all the stockings; then turned with a jerk,
And laying his finger aside of his nose,
And giving a nod, up the chimney he rose;

He sprang to his sleigh,
 to his team gave a whistle,
And away they all flew
 like the down of a thistle.
But I heard him exclaim,
 ere he drove out of sight,

Happy Christmas to All and to All a Good Night!